THIS LAND CALLED AMERICA: KANSAS

CREATIVE EDUCATION

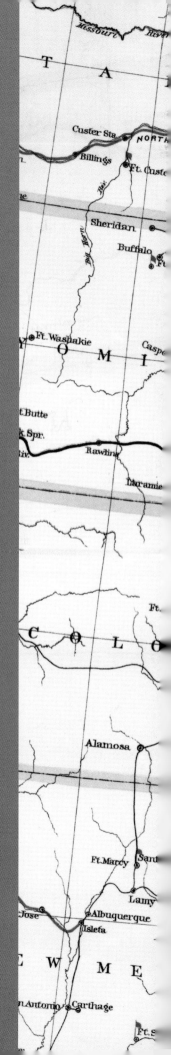

Published by Creative Education
P.O. Box 227, Mankato, Minnesota 56002
Creative Education is an imprint of The Creative Company
www.thecreativecompany.us

Book and cover design by Blue Design (www.bluedes.com)
Art direction by Rita Marshall
Printed in the United States of America

Photographs by Corbis (Bettmann, Chris Rainier), Getty Images (Slim
Aarons, Altrendo images, Altrendo nature, American Stock, Archive
Holdings Inc., Ingo Arndt, Ed Clark//Time Life Pictures, H. F. Davis/
Topical Press Agency, English School, Kyle Gerstner, Jeri Gleiter, Hulton
Archive, MGM Studios, MPI, Charles Ommanney, Jim Reed, Baron
Dudevant Jean Maurice San, Philip Schermeister/National Geographic,
Larry W. Smith, VisionsofAmerica/Joe Sohm, Hank Walker//Time Life
Pictures)

Library of Congress Cataloging-in-Publication Data
Labairon, Cassandra.
Kansas / by Cassandra Labairon.
p. cm. — (This land called America)
Includes bibliographical references and index.
ISBN 978-1-58341-641-9
1. Kansas—Juvenile literature. I. Title. II. Series.
F681.3.L33 2008
978.1—dc22   2007015009

First Edition
9 8 7 6 5 4 3 2 1

This Land Called America

KANSAS

Cassandra Labairon

THIS LAND CALLED AMERICA

Kansas

CASSANDRA LABAIRON

EACH SPRING, AFTER THE SNOW MELTS AND THE WARM WINDS BEGIN TO BLOW, KANSAS FARMS COME ALIVE WITH ACTIVITY. FARMERS RUMBLE ACROSS THE FIELDS IN THEIR LARGE TRACTORS. THEY SOW THE SEEDS FOR WHEAT, CORN, AND OTHER GRAINS. OVER THE LONG, HOT SUMMER, CROPS ALL OVER THIS PRAIRIE STATE GROW STRONG AND RIPEN. THEN, IN THE FALL, WHEN THE FIELDS HAVE CHANGED FROM GREEN TO GOLDEN, IT IS TIME FOR THE HARVEST. THE BUSY AUTUMN COUNTRYSIDE SIGNALS TO OBSERVERS THAT, ONCE AGAIN, KANSAS FARMERS HAVE GROWN FOOD THAT WILL FEED PEOPLE AND ANIMALS ALL OVER THE WORLD.

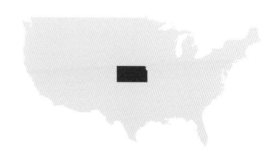

YEAR

1541   Spanish explorer Francisco Vásquez de Coronado discovers Indian villages in Kansas.

EVENT

Wild Prairie Home

Before Kansas became a state, it was home to many American Indian tribes. Tribes such as the Osage, Kansa, and Pawnee were Kansas's first farmers. They saved the seeds from the plants they gathered. Then they planted them in fields close to their homes. Some tribes hunted buffalo on the plains. Many of these tribes moved from place to place to follow the buffalo herds.

At one time, there were about 75 million buffalo living in the United States. The wild buffalo were important to the tribes in the Kansas area. Other wildlife that was plentiful before settlers came included prairie chickens, quail, turkeys, and deer.

In 1540, Spanish explorer Francisco Vásquez de Coronado left Mexico with an army to search for the fabled "Seven Golden Cities of Cíbola," which were supposed to contain treasures and gold. Instead, he found several humble Indian villages throughout the American southwest and Kansas. In 1803, the U.S. bought Kansas as part of the Louisiana Purchase

The American Indians (above) who first lived in Kansas used materials from animals such as buffalo (opposite) for clothing and ornamentation.

YEAR

1803   The U.S. acquires Kansas as part of the Louisiana Purchase.

EVENT

- 7 -

Kansas proved to be an
important battleground
in the fight between
North and South over
slavery.

from France. The U.S. promised the Indians who were living there that the land would be left to the native tribes. But by the 1850s, those promises were being ignored.

The Kansas territory was opened for settlement in 1854. Trappers, traders, soldiers, and cowboys moved to Kansas in search of wealth and adventure. Missionaries came to set up churches and schools. Farmers and business people also staked claims in Kansas. Soon, people were spread out all over the territory's prairie land.

On January 29, 1861, Kansas was admitted into the union as America's 34th state. The city of Topeka became its capital. Three months later, the Civil War started. Although it was a new state, Kansas sent men to fight for the Union, or Northern, army.

In 1867, the Union Pacific Railroad reached Abilene, Kansas. Because of the railroad, Abilene became an important town for ranchers. Ranchers organized cattle drives that traveled from Texas to the grasslands of Kansas. The route came to be known as the Chisholm Trail. After grazing along the trail, the fattened longhorn cattle were loaded onto railroad cars in Abilene to be shipped around the country.

YEAR
1830   The Indian Removal Bill uproots the area's native tribes from their homes.
EVENT

Kansas was a wild and lawless place in the late 1800s. Its citizens needed lawmen to keep the peace. Wyatt Earp was a famous lawman in Wichita and Dodge City. James Butler "Wild Bill" Hickok became Abilene's marshal, or top law-man, in 1871. Later, Hickok became an entertainer and traveled all over the world. He told stories about the exciting days of the Wild West.

Wild Bill Hickok was best known for his marksmanship, or how accurately he could shoot a gun.

As the 1800s ended and the 20th century began, wheat farming became popular, bringing farmers to Kansas. In the 1920s, coal, oil, and natural gas were discovered. This created more jobs. In the 1930s, big dust storms destroyed Kansas's crops. A lack of rain, combined with overuse of the land, turned the soil into a fine powder. When heavy winds came, the swirling dirt caused animals and people to suffer—and some even died during the "black blizzards."

Because of the dust storms of the 1930s, farmers had to learn new techniques. Also, Franklin Delano Roosevelt, the U.S. president at that time, encouraged people to start environmental conservation programs that would help Kansas recover and make sure that the damage the storms had caused never happened again.

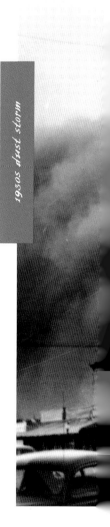

1930s dust storm

YEAR
1854   The Kansas-Nebraska Act creates the new territories of Kansas and Nebraska.
EVENT

Right in the Middle

America's agricultural industry, but it is also the geographic heart of the 48 contiguous states. Kansas is bordered by Nebraska to the north and Oklahoma to the south. Missouri borders Kansas on its eastern edge, and Colorado is on its western side.

In 1874, people from Russia moved to Kansas. They brought a new kind of wheat seed with them. By the beginning of the 1900s, Kansas had become a top wheat-producing state. It earned the nicknames "The Wheat State" and the "Breadbasket of America." Kansas grain is today sold not only in the U.S. but around the world.

The Wheat State can be divided into three regions: the Dissected Till Plains, the Southern Plains, and the Great Plains. The Dissected Till Plains area, in the northeastern part of the state, was formed by a glacier more than 400,000 years ago. The soil there is rich and good for crops.

The Southern Plains are split into two smaller sections known as the Osage Plains and the Flint Hills. People can see native prairie grasses and plants such as big bluestem in the Flint Hills area. The western half of the state is covered by the Great Plains. The highest point in Kansas is found there in the midst of a farmer's field. Mount Sunflower is 4,039 feet (1,232 m) above sea level, but it is not noticeably different from the surrounding landscape. It is a flat plain marked by an elevation sign, an American flag, and a metal sculpture of a sunflower.

Kansas produces the most wheat out of any state in America today, but North Dakota is a close second.

To get to Kansas, many people took covered wagons and traveled with all their animals and belongings.

Five major rivers run through Kansas: the Kansas, Arkansas, Missouri, Republican, and the Smoky Hill. The two largest lakes in the state are the Milford Reservoir and Tuttle Creek Lake. Bass, bluegills, flathead catfish, and walleye are some of the fish found in Kansas lakes and streams.

Eighty million years ago, Kansas was covered by an inland sea. Until the last ice age, the sea would come and go, and each time, the receding water would leave behind a layer of fossils. In the 1800s, scientists who studied fossils traveled to Kansas looking for these ancient remains. They discovered a wide variety of fossils, from mammoths to prehistoric birds and ancient sea life.

The Delaware River (opposite) is a northeastern branch of the Kansas River, a major waterway that runs through the state capital of Topeka (above, 1869).

Kansas is the first state to adopt prohibition, making it illegal to sell and consume alcohol.

After wheat has been
harvested, the seeds
from the grain are put
into grain elevators for
safe storage.

Harvested wheat field

Kansas has many natural resources. Petroleum, natural gas, salt, and coal are a few of the resources that are drilled for or mined in Kansas. The state is also a leader in the production of helium gas and construction materials, such as cement.

Kansas farmers grow one-fifth of all wheat produced in the U.S. They also grow sorghums, corn, soybeans, and a variety of other crops. Sorghums are grassy stalks grown for their nutritional, high-protein seeds. Animals eat sorghum grain, while corn and soybeans are used by both animals and people.

Because Kansas is flat, it is a windy state, and Dodge City is one of the windiest cities in America. During the hot summers, when temperatures usually climb above 90 °F (32 °C), Kansas sees many tornados and floods. Kansas is in "tornado alley," a section of the U.S. where large tornados can develop. In the winter, when temperatures drop to the teens or single digits, similar high winds can create severe blizzards. Occasional dust storms still hurt Kansas farmers' crops.

Buyers can go inside pens at stockyards to get a close-up view of the steers they want to purchase.

YEAR
1887   One of the world's largest salt deposits is discovered in Hutchinson.
EVENT

Pioneers and Poets

In the late 1820s, wagon trains brought settlers to Kansas. Because of the rich farmland and the easy access to railroads, "cow towns" such as Abilene sprang up. By the 1870s, Kansas was home to many farmers and cowboys. Many of the stories about Wild West gunfighters and outlaws come from 19th-century Kansas.

In 1862, President Abraham Lincoln signed the Homestead Act. It granted settlers free land as long as they built a home and lived on the land for five years. The Homestead Act brought settlers to Kansas from other states and countries such as Great Britain, Germany, and Sweden.

In the 1870s, after the Civil War had ended, many freed slaves moved to Kansas. Former slave Benjamin "Pap" Singleton started a colonizing plan to get more African Americans to move to Kansas. His plan was a success, and by 1880, more than 50,000 Southern blacks had moved to Kansas and a number of states farther north.

When the West was first opened to settlers, people raced across the plains to find a good piece of land.

Much has changed since the early days of Kansas cow towns, but modern cowboys still drive cattle.

Some ranches in Kansas are not for cattle but instead are home to herds of rare wild mustangs.

In the 1880s, many Croatians from eastern Europe came to Kansas seeking work. Danish, Italian, Russian, and Mexican immigrants also came to Kansas looking for a better way of life. Agriculture remained Kansas' main occupation until the 1920s.

Around 1920, advances in farming machinery required humans to do less of the labor. Jobs outside of agriculture become more available as towns sprouted up all over the state. By the year 2000, fewer than 30 percent of Kansas's residents lived in rural areas.

Today, many Kansans are employed by aerospace companies such as the Cessna Aircraft Company and Learjet Inc. Other major businesses include meat packing, mining, flour milling, and petroleum refining. Kansas leads the country in wheat and beef production. The state makes billions of dollars each year in the production, processing, and distribution of food.

Many notable people have ties to Kansas. The 34th U.S. president, Dwight D. Eisenhower, was born in Texas in 1890, but two years later, his family moved to Abilene, Kansas, where he was raised. Eisenhower was a famous general in World War II. Later, he supported civil rights. He believed that children of all races should be able to attend the same schools and that all Americans should have the right to vote.

Wichita Boeing plant

YEAR

1912   Kansas women win the right to vote eight years before the 19th amendment grants all American women the right.

EVENT

Today, the Boeing plant in Wichita focuses on producing aircraft and parts for the U.S. military.

YEAR

1932   Atchison native Amelia Earhart makes her first solo transatlantic flight.

EVENT

Dwight Eisenhower (pictured with wife Mamie) was an early supporter of the interstate highway system.

Amelia Earhart was born in Atchison, Kansas, in 1897. She was the first woman issued a pilot's license by the National Aeronautics Association. As a passenger on a 1928 transatlantic flight, Earhart became the first female to make the long trip across the Atlantic Ocean by air. In 1932, she made the flight solo, becoming the first woman pilot to do so. Sadly, in 1937, while attempting a historic flight around the world, Earhart and her plane disappeared.

YEAR
1952   Dwight D. Eisenhower becomes the first Kansan to be elected U.S. president.
EVENT

Gwendolyn Brooks

Kansas wheat field

A number of influential writers were born in Kansas. African American poet Gwendolyn Brooks was born in Topeka in 1917. In 1950, she became the first African American to win the Pulitzer Prize for poetry. William Stafford, another poet, grew up in Kansas and attended the University of Kansas at Lawrence. He wrote more than 65 books of poetry and prose and won many awards. Both Brooks and Stafford served as a consultant in poetry to the Library of Congress, a position now known as poet laureate.

Although poet Gwendolyn Brooks (above) grew up around the wheat fields (opposite) near Topeka, she later moved to Chicago, Illinois, where her work was first published.

1954   A Topeka case prompts the U.S. Supreme Court to rule that school segregation is unconstitutional.

Museums and Magic

THERE ARE MANY MUSEUMS AND PLACES OF INTEREST IN KANSAS. THE UNIVERSITY OF KANSAS IN LAWRENCE FEATURES THE NATURAL HISTORY MUSEUM AND THE SPENCER MUSEUM OF ART. THE NATURAL HISTORY MUSEUM HOUSES A VARIETY OF FOSSILS. THE SPENCER MUSEUM EXHIBITS ART FROM ALL OVER THE WORLD, BUT THE LARGEST COLLECTION OF AMERICAN ART IN THE STATE IS FOUND AT THE WICHITA ART MUSEUM.

The Kansas State Historical Society helps preserve the state's monuments, historic sites, and museums. Two of the museums they take care of are the Pawnee Indian Museum and the Native American Heritage Museum. The Pawnee Indian museum is located in north-central Kansas, near the town of Republic. The site features a Pawnee Indian lodge and artifacts. The Native American Heritage Museum in Highland displays artwork of the Great Lakes Indians who were forced to move to Kansas from states farther east in the 1800s.

The Kansas Cosmosphere and Space Center allows people to get a close-up look at spacecraft.

Hutchinson is the home of the Kansas Cosmosphere and Space Center. This space museum takes visitors on a tour of the history of space travel and other advances that occurred in the 20th century. The center also has an IMAX theater, live science shows, and a planetarium where visitors can learn about stars and the solar system in interactive ways.

Topeka's state capitol (above) may be recognizable only to Kansans, but all Americans think of Kansas when they see THE WIZARD OF OZ *(opposite).*

Another site that is unique to Kansas is in Cawker City. This small town is home to the world's largest ball of twine. The ball was started by a farmer in 1953. Today, the towns-people keep the ball of twine going every year at the town's annual Twine-A-Thon. Currently, the total twine length is well over seven million feet (2,133,600 m).

Kansas came into the spotlight in 1900 when L. Frank Baum published his children's book *The Wonderful Wizard of Oz*. In the story, a Kansas farm girl named Dorothy gets swept up by a tornado and lands on a yellow brick road in the magical land of Oz. The best-selling book was made into a movie in 1939. People all over the world still watch the movie and read the book today. People also visit the Oz Museum in Wamego, Kansas.

The inland sea that used to cover Kansas and other parts of the Midwest left behind towering chalk formations. Monument Rocks and Castle Rock are so breathtaking and unique that they were both named Natural National Landmarks by the U.S. government.

Instead of professional sports, many Kansans are devoted to powerhouse college teams such as the Jayhawks of the University of Kansas in Lawrence. Those who crave professional action follow the teams based in nearby Kansas City, Missouri. Located only 10 miles (16 km) from the Kansas-Missouri state line, Kansas City's Truman Sports Complex is home to three

YEAR
1961 Omar Kneclik of Coffeyville invents the first Icee machine for making frozen carbonated drinks, or slushies.
EVENT

1994   Kansas's Heartland Sustainable Agriculture Network helps farmers produce food while taking care of the land.

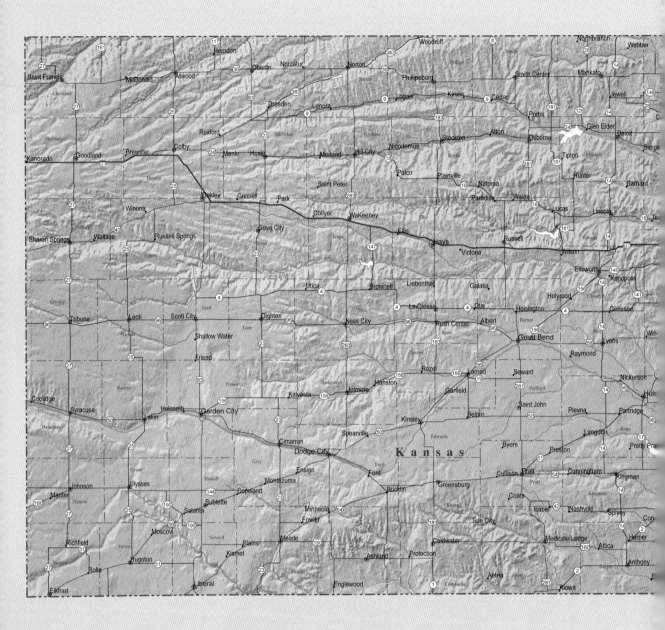

QUICK FACTS

Population: 2,764,075

Largest city: Wichita (pop. 354,617)

Capital: Topeka

Entered the union: January 29, 1861

Nicknames: Sunflower State, Breadbasket of America

State flower: sunflower

State bird: western meadowlark

Size: 82,277 sq mi (213,096 sq km)—15th-biggest in U.S.

Major industries: agriculture, aircraft and automobile manufacturing

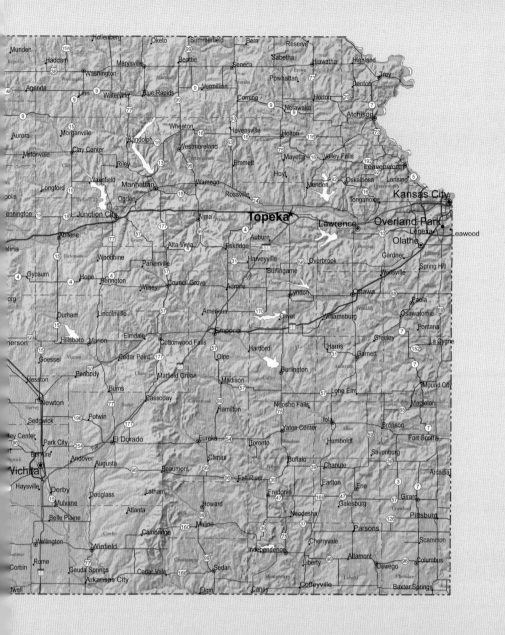

pro teams: the Royals of Major League Baseball, the Chiefs of the National Football League, and the Wizards of Major League Soccer.

From Mount Sunflower in the west and across the prairies to the east, Kansas offers an amazing view of earth and sky as far as the eye can see. The state's rich farming history has made it into the Breadbasket of America. The prairies, rolling hills, and exciting cities are home to many, and like Dorothy in *The Wizard of Oz*, many Kansans agree that "there's no place like home."

YEAR

2007 A tornado destroys 95 percent of the small town of Greensburg, Kansas, on May 4.

EVENT

BIBLIOGRAPHY

Ciovacco, Justine, Kathleen A. Feeley, and Kristen Behrens. *State-by-State Atlas*. New York: DK Publishing, 2003.

Gutman, Bill. *The Look-It-Up Book of the 50 States*. New York: Random House, 2002.

Kansas State Historical Society. "Homepage." Kansas Historical Society. http://www.kshs.org/.

King, David C. *Children's Encyclopedia of American History*. New York: DK Publishing, 2003.

Mead, Robin, Polly Mead, and Andrew Gutelle. *Our National Parks*. New York: Smithmark, 1992.

Young, Donald, and Cynthia Overbeck Bix. *Our National Parks*. San Francisco: Sierra Club Books, 1990.

INDEX